Animal Peculiarity Volume 2 Part 4

By T.P Just
~~~

Get All The Books In The Series:

Animal Peculiarity Volume 1 [1-8]
Animal Peculiarity Volume 2 [1-8]
Just Enterprises

I0436333

Table of Contents

1. Prologue

THERE is perhaps nothing extraordinary in the fact that man is wise and just, takes great care to provide for his own children, -shows due consideration for his parents, seeks sustenance for himself, protects himself against plots, and possesses all the other gifts of nature which are his. For man has been endowed with speech, of all things the most precious, and has been granted reason, which is of the greatest help and use.

Moreover, he knows how to reverence and worship the gods. But that dumb animals should by nature possess some good quality and should have many of man's amazing excellences assigned to them along with man, is indeed a remarkable fact. And to know accurately the special characteristics of each, and how living creatures also have been a source of interest no less than man, demands a trained intelligence and much learning. Now I am well aware of the labour that others have expended on this subject, yet I have collected all the materials that I could; I have clothed them in untechnical language, and am persuaded that my achievement is a treasure far from negligible. So if anyone considers them profitable, let him make use of them; anyone who does not consider them so may give them to his father to keep and attend to.

For not all things give pleasure to all men, nor do all men consider all subjects worthy of study. Although I was born later than many accomplished writers of an earlier day, the accident of date ought not to mulct me of praise, if I too produce a learned work whose ampler research and whose choice of language make it deserving of serious attention.

2. The Duck

When the Duck lays its eggs it lays them on land but close to a lake or shallow pool or some other watery, moist spot. And the Duckling by some mysterious instinct knows that it is incapable both of flying high in the air and of remaining on land.

For this reason it leaps into the water and can swim from the moment it is hatched; it has no need to learn but dives and comes up again with great skill as though it had already been taught for some time.

3. And Eagle

But the Eagle which they call the 'duck-killer' swoops upon the Duck as she swims, meaning to carry her off; but the Duck dives and vanishes, and then after swimming under water, bobs up in another place.

But the Eagle is there also, and again the Duck dives; and this happens again and again. Then one of two things follows: either the Duck after a dive is drowned, or the Eagle goes off after other prey; whereupon the Duck, with nothing to fear, swims once more upon the surface.

4. The Swan and death

The Swan has this advantage over men in matters of the greatest moment, for it knows when the end of its life is at hand, and, what is more, in bearing its approach with cheerfulness, it has received from Nature the noblest of gifts. For it is confident that in death there is neither pain nor sorrow. But men are afraid of what they know not, and regard death as the greatest of all ills.

Now the Swan has so contented a spirit that at the very close of its life it sings and breaks out into a dirge, as it were, for itself. Even so does Euripides sing of Bellerophon, prepared like a hero of high soul for death. For example, he has portrayed him addressing his soul thus.

'Reverent wast thou ever in life towards the gods; strangers didst not thou succour; nor didst thou ever grow weary towards thy friends'- and so on. So then the Swan too intones its own funeral chant and either by hymns to the gods or by the rehearsal of its own praises it makes provision for its departure.

Socrates also testifies to the fact that it sings not from sorrow but rather from cheerfulness, for (he says) a man whose heart is vexed and sore has no leisure for song and melody.

Now death is not the only thing that the Swan faces with courage: it is not afraid of a fight. But though it will not be the first to do an injury, any more than a sober, educated man would be, yet it will not retire and give way before an aggressor.

While all other birds are on terms of peace with the Swan, the Eagle has frequently attacked it, as Aristotle says , though it has never yet overcome it, but has always been defeated not only through the strength of the Swan in battle but also because in defending itself the Swan has justice on its side.

5. The Heron and oysters

The Heron is a great eater of oysters and swallows them when closed, as pelicans swallow mussels. And the Heron warms the oysters a little in what is called its 'crop' and retains them there.
Under the influence of the heat the oysters open, and the Heron becoming aware of this, disgorges the shells but retains the flesh; and it lives by consuming entire, thanks to a strong digestion, all that passes down into it.

6. The Asterias

There is a bird called Asterias (starling?) and in Egypt, if tamed, it understands human speech. And if anyone by way of insult calls it 'slave,' it gets angry; and if anyone calls it 'skulker,' it takes umbrage and is annoyed, as though it was being jeered at for its low birth and rebuked for its indolence.

The Torpedo

If a man with the juice of silphium on his hands seizes the Torpedo, he avoids the pain which it inflicts.

7. The Great Weever

And should you attempt to draw the Great Weever from the sea with your right hand, it will not come but will fight vigorously. But if you haul it up with your left hand, it yields and is captured.

8. The Nightingale

From a statement of Charmis of Massilia I learn that the Nightingale is fond of music, and even fond of fame. At any rate when it is singing to itself in lonely places, he says, its melody is simple and spontaneous. But in captivity when it has no lack of hearers it lifts up its voice, warbling and trilling its melting music. And Homer seems to me to hint as much when he says.

'And as when the daughter of Pandareus, the greenwood Nightingale, sings sweet at the first oncoming of spring, as she rests amid the thick leafage of the trees, and ever varying her note pours forth her full-throated music.'

9. The Lion

Democritus asserts that the Lion alone among animals is born with its eyes open and from the hour of birth is already to some extent angry and ready to perform some spirited action. And others have observed that even when asleep the Lion moves his tail, showing, as you might expect, that he is not altogether quiescent, and that, although sleep has enveloped and enfolded him, it has not subdued him as it does all other animals.

The Egyptians, they say, claim to have observed in him something of this kind, asserting that the Lion is superior to sleep and forever awake.

And I have ascertained that it is for this reason that they assign him to the sun, for, as you know, the sun is the most hard-working of the gods, being visible above the earth or pursuing his course beneath it without pause.

And the Egyptians cite Homer as a witness when he speaks of the 'untiring sun'. And in addition to his strength the Lion shows intelligence. For instance, he has designs upon cattle and goes to their folds by night. Now Homer was aware of this when he said

'Like cattle which a lion has scared, coming in the dead of night.'

And his Prey

And he strikes terror into them all by his strength, but seizes only one and devours it. And when he has gorged himself, he wishes to preserve the remains for another occasion, yet he is ashamed to stay and watch over them, as though he were afraid of starving from want of food.

Accordingly with jaws agape he breathes upon them and trusts to his breath to guard them while he himself goes on his way. But when the other beasts arrive and realise to whom the remains upon the ground belong, they do not venture to touch them but go their way for fear of seeming to rob and diminish anything that belongs to their king.

Now if the Lion chances to be lucky and has good hunting, he forgets his former prize, disregards it as being stale, and goes away. Otherwise he returns to it as to a private store. And when he has eaten more than enough, he empties himself by lying quiet and abstaining from food, or alternatively he catches a monkey and eats some of it, voiding and emptying his belly by means of its flesh.

The Lion is after all upright and one to 'defend himself against the man who should assail him first'

Thus, he faces his attacker and by lashing with his tail and Winding it about his flanks rouses himself as though he were stimulating himself with a spur. And if a man shoot at him but miss him, he will defend himself by a fair return: he will scare the man but do him no harm.

The Lion tamed

If he has been domesticated since the time when he was a cub, he is extremely gentle and agreeable to meet, and is fond of tamed play, and will submit with good temper to any treatment to please his keeper. For instance, Hanno kept a Lion to carry his baggage; a tame Lion was the companion of Berenice and was no different from her tiring-slaves: for example, it would softly wash her face with its tongue and smooth away her wrinkles; it would share her table and eat in a sober, orderly fashion just like a man. And Onomarchus, the Tyrant of Catana, and the son of Cleomenes both had Lions with them as table-companions.

10. The Leopard

They say that the Leopard has a marvelous fragrance about it. To us it is imperceptible, though the Leopard is aware of the advantage it possesses, and other animals besides share with it this knowledge and the Leopard catches them in the following manner. When the Leopard needs food it conceals itself in a dense thicket or in deep foliage and is in- visible; it only breathes. And so fawns and gazelles and Wild goats and suchlike animals are drawn by the Spell, as it were, of its fragrance and come close up. Whereat the Leopard springs out and seizes its prey.

11. Honey of Various Kinds

And they say that all over Cappadocia the Bees produce honey without combs, and the story goes that it is thick like oil. I am informed that at Trapezus in Pontus honey is obtained from box-trees, finds but that it has a heavy scent and drives healthy people out of their senses, but restores the frenzied to health.

I learn that in Media honey drips from the trees, just as Euripides says that on Cithaeron sweet drops flow from the boughs. In Thrace too I have heard that honey is produced from plants. On Myconus there are no bees, and moreover if imported from outside they die.

The 'Day-Fly'

Aristotle says that on the banks of the river Hypanis there occurs a creature that goes by the name of 'day-fly,' because it is born in the morning twilight and dies when the sun begins to set.

The Cuttle-fish

The Cuttle-fish has a poisonous bite and teeth that are concealed very deep within. It seems also that the Osmylus and the Octopus are given to biting. And the Octopus has a more powerful bite than the Cuttle-fish, although it emits less poison.

12. The Wild Boar

They say that the Wild Boar does not attack The Wild a man until he has whetted his tusks. And Homer testifies to this when he says: 'Having whetted the white tusk between his curved jaws.'

And I learn that the Boar fattens himself chiefly by not washing but spending his time wallowing in the mud, drinking the turbid water, and reveling in the quiet and the darkness of his lair and in all the more inflating foods that can fill him up.

And Homer appears to imply as much, for touching their wallowing and their fondness for the more muddy ponds . . . when he says 'hogs that make their bed upon the ground.' And that they fatten themselves upon turbid water . . . he says 'Drinking black water, which fosters the rich fat on swine.' And that they delight in darkness he proves in the following words.' They slumbered beneath a hollow rock under shelter from Boreas.'

And he hints at the inflating quality of their food when he says that they eat 'the satisfying acorn.' Now Homer knowing that the Boar grows thin and that his flesh wastes if he looks at the Sow, has described the Boars as sleeping in one place and the Sows in another.

In Salamis if a Sow breaks in and grazes the corn when green or a field of waving corn, there is a law of the Salaminians that her teeth must be destroyed. And they say that the passage in Homer about 'a sow that consumes the crops' refers to this. Others take a different view and assert that when a Sow has tasted green corn its teeth are weakened.

13. Nature's medicines for animals

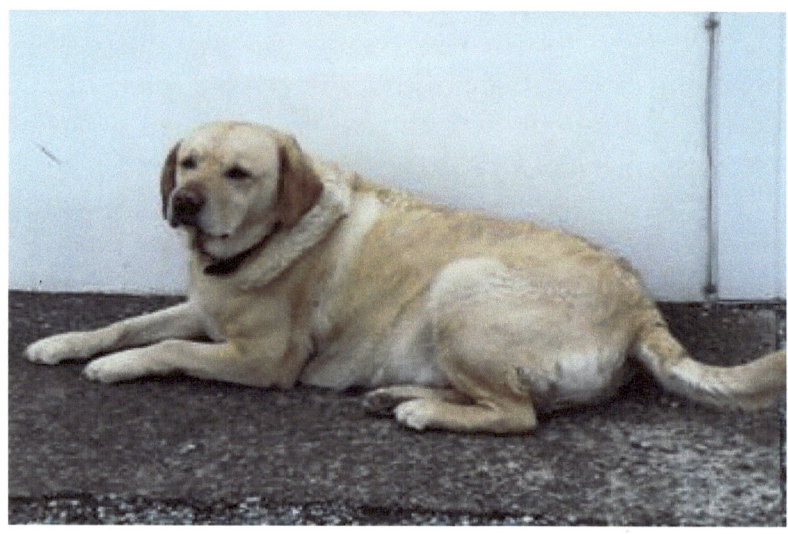

It would appear that Nature has provided grass as a remedy for the wounds of Dogs. And if they are troubled with worms they get rid of them by eating 'standing' corn, as it is called. And when they need to empty both stomachs "they are said to eat some grass, and as much of their food as remains undigested they vomit up, While the remainder is excreted. It is from this source that the Egyptians are said to have learnt the practice of taking purges. But Partridges, Storks, and Ring-doves, when wounded are said to chew marjoram and then to spread it on their wounds and cure their body; and they have no need' at all of man's healing art.
In this matter I shall have no need of any witness from antiquity but shall narrate what I myself have seen and know.

14. A Lizard, blinded, regains its sight.

A man captured a Lizard of the excessively green and unusually large species, and with a point made of bronze he pierced and blinded the Lizard.

And after boring some very fine holes in a newly fashioned earthenware vessel so as to admit the air, but small enough to prevent the creature from escaping, he heaped some very moist earth into it and put the Lizard inside together with a certain herb, of which he did not divulge the name, and an iron ring with a bezel of lignite engraved with the figure of a lizard.

After stamping nine seals upon the vessel he then covered it up, removing one seal daily for nine days. And when he had destroyed the last seal of all he opened the vessel, and I myself saw the Lizard having its sight and its eyes, which till then had been blinded, seeing perfectly well.

And we released the Lizard on the spot where it had been captured, and the man who had done these things asserted that, that ring of his was good for the eyes.

15. Animal friendships and enmities

It fills me with shame, you human beings, to think of the friendly relations that subsist between animals, not only those that feed together nor even those of the same species, but even between those that have no connexion through a common origin.

For instance, Sheep are friends with Goats; there is friendship between Pigeon and Turtle-dove; Ring- doves and Partridges entertain friendly feelings towards one another; We have long known that the Halcyon and the Ceryl desire each other; that the Crow is friendly disposed towards the Heron, and the Sea-mew towards the Little Cormorant, as it is called, and the Shearwater towards the Kite.

But there is war everlasting and without truce, so to say, between Crows and Owls. Enemies too are the Kite and the Raven, the Pyrallis and the Turtle-dove, the Bren- thus and the Sea-mew, and again the Greenfinch (?) and the Turtle-dove, the Aegypius and the Eagle, Swans and Water-snakes and Lions are the enemies of Antelopes and Bulls.

The bitterest hate exists between the Elephant and the Python," between the Asp and the Ichneumon, between the Blue Tit and the Ass, for directly the Ass brays the Blue Tit's eggs are smashed and the young ones are spilt, still imperfect. And so to avenge its offspring the Blue Tit leaps upon the Ass's sore places and feeds on them.

The Fox detests a Falcon and the Bull a Raven, and the Buff-backed Heron the Horse. And an educated man who attends to what he hears should know that the Dolphin is at feud with the Whale, the Basse too with the Mullet, and the Moray with the Conger Eel, and so on.

16. Animals dislike of dead bodies

When Bears have sniffed at hunters who have fallen on their face and knocked the breath out of themselves, they leave them for dead, and it seems that these creatures are disgusted by a dead body, Mice also hate those that die in their holes and lurking- places; and a Swallow too ejects a dead Swallow from its nest.

Ants also, thanks to the supreme wisdom of Nature, are careful to carry away dead bodies and to cleanse their nests, for it is characteristic of brute beasts that, when one of their own species and kind has died, they speedily remove it out of sight.

17. The various sounds made by animals

Nature has made animals with an immense variety of voice and of speech, as it were, even as she has men. For instance, the Scythian speaks one language, the Indian another; the Ethiopian has a natural language, so too have the Sacae; the language of Greece and that of Rome are different.
And so it is with animals: each has a different Way of producing the tone and the sound natural to its tongue. Thus, one roars, another lows, a third whinnies, (another) brays, yet another baas and bleats ; while to some howling is customary, to others barking, and to another snarling.
Screaming, whistling, booting, and singing, warbling, twittering, and countless other gifts of Nature are peculiar to different animals.

Animals Suckling their young

The lamb, the kid, and every foal directly it is born goes for its dam's teats and sucks the dugs until it is full. And the parent shows no concern but stands still. Whereas all animals with parted toes, wolves, hounds, lions, leopards, lie down to, give their young suck.

18. Reptiles foretell and avoid the rising of the Nile

In the Egyptian countryside Asps have their holes by the Nile on either bank. Most of the times they stay round about their (lurking-places) and are as attached to them as human beings are to their own homes.

But when in the summertime the river threatens to over flow, the aforesaid Asps emigrate some thirty days beforehand to districts further away from the Nile and creep into bluffs above the river, and, what is more, bring their young with them: they have received from Nature this special gift of being able to foretell the annual visitation of a river so mighty and so active, and to guard against being overtaken and destroyed by it.

And at the same season turtles and crabs and crocodiles transfer their eggs to spots which the river cannot touch or reach. Hence those who come across the eggs of the aforesaid creatures calculate to what extent the Nile will rise and irrigate their land.

19. The Hippopotamus

Hippopotamuses are nursling's of the Nile, and when the crops are ripe and the ears are yellow they do not forthwith begin to graze and eat them but pass along outside the crop and calculate what area will satisfy them; and then, having reckoned how much will be enough, they fall to, and as they fill themselves they withdraw backwards, keeping the river behind them.

Now this move they have cleverly devised so that, should any farmers attack them in self defence, they can run down into the water with complete ease, on the lookout for enemies in front of them but not looking behind them.

20. Leopard and Monkeys

In Mauretania Leopards do not attack Monkeys with force nor
with all the strength and power at their command, the reason
being that the Monkeys do not face them but escape from
them and run up trees and sit there on guard against the
designs of the Leopards.

Yet it seems that after the entire Leopard is craftier than the
Monkey, for such designs and traps does it contrive for the
Monkeys. It comes to the place where a gathering of Monkeys
is seated, throws itself down beneath a tree, lies on the ground
on its back, inflates its belly, relaxes its legs, closes both eyes,
and even holds its breath, and lies there like one dead.

And the Monkeys looking down upon their most hated
enemy, fancy it to be dead; and what they most fervently
desire, that they believe. For all that, they do not as yet take
courage but make an experiment, and the experiment is this
they send down one of their number whom they regard as the
most fearless to test and to scrutinise the state of the Leopard.

So the Monkey descends not altogether unafraid; but after running down a little way he turns back, fear causing him to retreat. And a second time he descends and having approached, withdraws; and a third time he returns and observes the Leopard's eyes and examines it to see if it is breathing.

But the Leopard, by remaining motionless with the utmost self-control, inspires a gradual fearlessness in the Monkey. And since it approaches and remains close by and takes no harm, the Monkeys up aloft also now gather courage and run down from that particular tree and from all others that grow nearby, and assembling in a mass encircle the Leopard and dance round it.

Then they leap upon it and turn somersaults on its body and by dancing in triumph a dance appropriate to monkeys, and by a variety of insults testify to the joy and delight they feel over the sup- posed corpse.

But the Leopard submits to all this until it realises that the Monkeys are tired by their dancing and their insolence, when it leaps up UN- expectedly and springs at them. And some it lacerates with its claws, others it tears to pieces with its teeth, and enjoys without stint the ample and sumptuous banquet provided by its enemies.

It is Nature that bids the Leopard endure with heroic fortitude, so that it may rise superior to the insults of its enemies, bearing up with the utmost patience and finding no need to say 'endure, my heart' .Indeed the son of Laertes was within an ace of revealing himself prematurely through being unable to tolerate the insults of the maidservants.

21. Deer crossing the sea

The Deer of Syria are born on the highest mountains, on Amanus, on Libanus, and on Carmel. And when they want to cross the sea the herd goes down to the beaches and waits until the wind drops; and as soon as they observe that there is a favourable and gentle breeze, then they brave the open sea. And they swim in single file, holding on to one another, the ones behind supporting their chins on the rumps of those in front . . .takes the last place in the line, and resting itself upon the one next in front of it in the whole troop, brings up the rear. And they make for Cyprus in their longing for the meadows there, for they are said to be deep and to afford excellent pasture.

The Cypriots indeed claim that they live in a fertile country, and venture to compare their arable land with that of Egypt. And there are Deer from other countries too which show this same capacity for swimming. For example, the Deer of Epirus swim across to Corcyra: the two countries face each other across a strait.

The Elephant

In India Elephants, when compelled by the natives to pull up some tree, roots and all, do not immediately attack it and begin the task, until they have shaken it and have tested it thoroughly to see whether in fact it can be overturned, or whether that is utterly impossible.

Get All The Books In The Series:

Animal Peculiarity Volume 1 [1-8]
Animal Peculiarity Volume 2 [1-8]

www.ingramcontent.com/pod-product-compliance
Lightning Source LLC
Chambersburg PA
CBHW050911290526
45792CB00002B/775